Stone Sky Lifting

WINNER OF THE 2000 OHIO STATE UNIVERSITY PRESS /
THE JOURNAL AWARD IN POETRY

Stone Sky Lifting

Lia Purpura

Ohio State University Press COLUMBUS

Library of Congress Cataloging-in-Publication Data
Purpura, Lia, 1964–
   Stone sky lifting / Lia Purpura.
      p.   cm.
   "Winner of the 2000 Ohio State University Press/
   The Journal Award in Poetry."
   ISBN 0-8142-0862-2 (alk. paper) — ISBN 0-8142-5065-3
   (pbk. : alk. paper)
   I. Title.
   PS3566.U67S76   2000
   811'.54—dc21
                  00-009093

Other identifiers: ISBN 978-0-8142-0862-5 (cloth) | ISBN 0-8142-
0862-2 (cloth) | ISBN 978-0-8142-5065-5 (paper) | ISBN 0-8142-
5065-3 (paper)

Text and jacket design by Wilsted & Taylor.
Type set in Deepdene by Wilsted & Taylor.

ACKNOWLEDGMENTS

*Grateful acknowledgment is made to the following publications
in which these poems first appeared:*

Antioch Review, "Accident"
Chelsea, "Shadow"
Cutbank, "Oath"
Iowa Review, "Red"
The Journal, "Agreement," "Dance," and "Disturbances"
New Letters, "At Six Months"
Ohio Review, "Some Solaces"
Parnassus: Poetry in Review, "Bee"
Passages North, "Project"
Ploughshares, "Cicada"
Prairie Schooner, "Milkweed," "Myth"
Seneca Review, "I Wanted the Sound"
Southern Review, "Beads"
Witness, "Grasses"

"Bee" was awarded the Randall Jarrell Poetry Prize
and also appeared in the *Maryland Millennial Anthology.*

My thanks to the MacDowell Colony and the Center
for Humanities at Loyola College for their generous
support of my work, and to Tina Barr, A. V. Christie,
and Jed Gaylin for their rigor, insight, and care.

CONTENTS

I

II

True solace is finding none, which is to say it is everywhere.

I

Bee

For once I was not bent
on denying the worst scenario
but listened to the bee
get louder as it came closer.
I was still as the rumble moved
into my chest and the machinery
of its wings passed over.

The bee kept changing direction, midair,
and the sound diminished or drew close randomly.
I've seen the brightest yellow flicker
do the same in a wet, green field
—take one sip, reverse itself,
and look for some fresh thing because
it so loved the idea of abundance.

But I was only part of the abundance.
And who else would I be
so adorned, but clearly
an attractive thing to it,
a singular sweetness
willing to think
like an ornament.

※

Then I saw myself as I was—
not nearly what it wanted.
I did not grow, like the rose,
dangerous and inviting
steps to my heart, and my heart
was not perfect—hidden,
dusty, and small.

※

In place of what it wanted,
I would do. And I saw
my two wild arms
in the air, waving,
not knowing how to say
I was more than that,
in its language.

Stone Birds

A stone is a grounded bird—
its blue wings are folded.
The small clefts there can be mended,
but only by attention.

It would like to find
the air again
a not-so-distant thing.

But the stone needs a wing to take it up
for a view of the road,
to make the road a ribbon, unspooling.

If the stone were a bird
with an eye for a draft,
it could fly with its wings
lashed to its body.

It would look like a tear,
a drop of rain, if the sky
were to open its black,
petalled wings.

If the sky were to drop
its petals of rain,

a bird would lose
the race to ground.
Would stop the race and catch a draft
up, like a stone hefted and flung.

Water would collect.
Black, in clefts,
on the grounded stone.

A bird would come and dip its head
down to drink. Quiet would grow.

And a stone in a river
would look up to see
a white bird in blue sky
disintegrate,
take its gauzy wings
and fold them
hard against its body,

fly with a message
and drop a sound down:

a thunderclap: stones
with wings flying about!

Stones with wings
beating the air.
Breaking it up,
sending blue bits into riverbeds.

From the river's view,
too few birds
have come today.
Too few have folded
into their wings
the flaws of ground:

they fly so lightly
over the water, over the stones,
where things are hidden.

The birds have forgotten
before air, before wings,
just who they were.

Without their song
what silence was,
and how it moved upon
the water.

About a time
when stones were islands
and water a ribbon
that lashed the distant lands together.

So the birds could call out to one another
and hear the news about the sky.

About the sky, stone gray, that knew
the hearts of birds, stone hearts,
before they knew
themselves.

Standing Figure
with Knife Edge

AFTER HENRY MOORE

The iron-cool and stationary bone.
Those marrow holes and hollows on the rump end turned
that I might look through, that I might see
how she became all vertebrae
and knife-fine pleat. How she made herself
a perfect solitude: no woman I know
escapes cleaning up, so she, too, must be
—at her age, on her knees.

And there, in the sun, at the end of August,
when heat is a force, oppressive as anger,
she in the courtyard, she the bone skirt
inclined to me. I had come to feel
this wedge of dark patience pass over.

I laid my head upon her bone-apron,
visibly creased to a humble edge,
and asked how many years it takes
to love the full weight of yourself
in a circumscribed courtyard.

I asked how to be as she was, with no cape
for the coming wind, no white deflection
from the sun.

I sat a long time while she ministered
to the light. She was everywhere
stunting all embellishment. And though
wind snagged in the steep pleats she wore,
she shed the wind's fingerings for silence.
She shed the need to be seen for presence.
She told me, soon, that I would be, with my new child,
more alone than I had ever been. And grateful for it.

The Eel's Fear

That disgust overcomes
the fact of my eyes,
the muscle of my body
so like the bent animal
of your arm.
That no one loves the pipe
of a throat, the shred
of a neck, a stiff embrace.
My slightest gestures
make holes in waves,
though I am a wave myself,
and close to the way you think
of pain as lashing,
instinctive and awful,
but in the end productive.
            You love the dust and dusty things
in your good moments
of simplicity: the butterfly
that barely grazes the tongues of flowers
and lightly leaves,
while I am all oil and hunger.
What else do I do
down there in the dark?
Think. What would you do?
Part with the body

another's resistance.
You have beautiful words for that:
undulating, grace, and *bearing.*
You give them to your women.
And the words for things
you give to your men,
machete and *scythe,*
I am those too. I don't know which
I like more—a way of being seen,
or being.
      If I could speak
beyond the S of my body,
I'd be the black fan
of a crow's call, that place
where fear and instinct meet.
It's the sound I make in my head,
and once made aloud,
at the flight of my babies from me,
those transparent ribbons of hope.
There were hundreds.

On Waiting

What is air
but a terrible fishhook
swallowed whole?

And the curve
of your back, striped
rind, path,

what, before you grew
in the cage I am: like faith:
cowl first, head next,

and fit my secret emptiness:
Why are the most violently bent trees
also a habit of growth?

And how does green come on
so softly
and deny that utterly?

At Six Months

Heavy things get seen like this—
not smart, not mean.
I know, I know, inside's a seed
growing, dividing, it should make me
kind in my roundness. It kicks
the heaviness I am, and I
take it all, absorb the blow, the current
circling out in rings: mother
to be, to be, to be: inside
isn't old enough to be known.
In a few more months, this counting
stops, and starts again on the clock's
black dot. Look, in the corner of the yard,
what used to be a weed is measured
in circumference now, whose leaves are broad
and full of intention, tipped
to let the rain course down
the determined path to the determined vein.
Today someone said *rest*,
you deserve it. What does that mean?
And who am I now
if I call that bloom a tree?

Myth

Once I believed nothing unintended
passed over my face.
That I was placid-seeming
as a flower, virtuosic
at being seen.

And I was indecorous
in other ways. I believed
I could live in harmony
with elemental shapes—
circles, for instance,

without a thought to revolution—
that I would make of them
wheels for a handcart. Proofs.
Halos, complete with crowds
of saints, upright.

Of the usual way the story moves,
from discontent to wandering to
deliverance, I did not believe
it was arrogant to keep wandering
all to myself.

I believed that pity,
abundant as rain, was born
of an impulse for charity.
And in the presence of the inexorable,
I wanted to be

the one to measure, cut, and drape,
to dress fate like a mannequin
and prop it up, so no one would know,
so I would not think
I was alone.

I will tell you I went down,
in all earnestness, to the cold,
clear water to see
what I'd made of myself.

There was the way I bent to drink,
there was the terrible grace of my neck.
And though I held very still
in the long gaze of embellishment,
what I saw could not be fixed
by falling in love with it.

I Wanted the Sound

I wanted the sound to be simple, I wanted
the deep rushing-over to come
from buckets let fly, that it just be the gutter
unhinged and singing, releasing
a tide, saying nothing as lasting
as *ramparts* or *glare*: but disaster's
eye is too beautifully clear: a garbage can
dragging and *dragged* would mean
my neighbor, fifteen, is out in the wet,
in the cold, cleaning up: that's how relief
startles: *better him than me*. That's how close
the sound came to my dream
of the passel of children—how a word
dumb as *passel* made them weightless, light-hearted,
though all four were in shackles, and I did
nothing, it was Poland, it was not
my language, I was lost in the station,
the shops were all selling
sweets, *Lebkuchen,*
it was summer, the chocolate was
melting, and all I could do
—it was not my language, no
coins for the train, no tokens or
tickets and every shop closing—was think:
get away, get away from them,

who weren't exactly unhappy in chains,
in collars, on leashes, dragged
up when they fell and what
could I do—it was Poland
again and over and over, I could not
find my way out of the station,
did not speak the language—but
what was the sound with its open mouth
saying, its scraping and timbre—*where
will you go, and who will you be,
without them, alone,
and safe, in that way?*

Oath

To do no harm beyond need and not to hurt.
To catch you up by the leg, to be
that body of doubt you denied always.
To graze your lifeline, tell the future only once.
To sharpen the knife till it's thin as a leaf.
To boil water, hide the rope.
To wear the scent of an unlocked gate.
To quiet the bucket's handle with a rag.
To let you eat in silence.
To compare your broad back to fresh lumber
and muscles to spring bulbs. To wait
to say your name aloud and clot your ear with sense.
To prepare my arms to reshape fear.
To catch your intelligent eye with mine.

To stand in the widening circle and soak my boots to the ankle.
To scrape wiry hair, to keep water boiling.
To hang the shell of you in waves of smoke.
To unpack a pot the size of your thoughts
and jars enough for the jewels of your insides.
To linger over pale pink ones.
To force hands in. To bloody my apron,
to isolate every fracture and pour salt over.
To break bones to go deeper, to empty my mind,
to make a tent of you, to balance the knife, to say

your eyes are as white as milk so almost blue.
To bring the wheel of my attention
and quick hands to the smallest bones
that articulated jumping. To tie
a second apron on. To wear myself out. To find
you blooming suds, to be the one to have fed you,
whose abundance is proof of my love.

Disturbances

The way the vine quivers

like an ear
listening
for a bird at the tangled center.

In winter, it measures

emptiness, the way a gaze lands
on the space below
that boy's pinned sleeve.

The question it sketches over and over—

whose body just now entered air,
and where did it go
with the bloom of its best idea?

Requiem

TO MY CHILD

Tap tap, like seconds piling, the robin stuffed quills of pine
      in the rafters, its beak plaited air, then *pock* in dry ground.
This was the morning measuring fear,
      the hours it took for the bird to make
of a cellophane wrapper a window, a floor,
      song in the shape of *safely graze,*
safe from hail, from sounds that sharpen in the grass
      and make the blades there real.
Of the same grass I walk easily over, that bird was working to
      stay above, stay above it, and sang of this work. I won't forget how
startling the moment it began, that low, breathy rumble
      when I turned the car on. How, driving off, I had no idea where
that lowest sound was issuing from—underneath, above, or trailing me?
      Of course it was. The insect sound
in the small space of the car, tape turning over,
      was somewhere, too, in the house this morning,
tap tap of finding the windowpane, more
      window than the wasp knew what to do with, dancing
along it, oddly dancing, a children's game, a child teasing:
      here, then gone. I was hearing all this, richest chords of
absence, entering the moving car, the children at play in the street near-
      missing and parting, each a map of wild intention,
and the morning held back in its history, black

seed-sized eyes, vines-turned-thatching, ready
for lashing, bones hollowed for flight, songs rising,
    a shadow at its labor, lengthening
as the bird worked straight through outside my window.
      But I was not there to watch it all. I went out. *We* went: that
        fact
repeated down the day: we were driving out of town,
    and heavy as I was with you, daylight rose.
Deep inside I felt you turn, as a bird
    flew down to the highway's island
(oh the rushing storm we were in, the divided
    sea of cars in flight on either side of the dividing line),
and there in the pine, I slowed to see, was the bird's heavy breast
    more modest this time, with coloring enough
—of rusty copper, silty run-off—to please the eye, not enough
    for death to want yet, death stalking the yard as it does,
      with industry,
stalking the highway with speed, intimate as an eye
    brimming, as I was, and hauling, oh I was
tired then and you were running
    into your own beginning, that looping
hiss loose in the car, a conflagration, blast of sun
    the trucks unleashed behind them as they moved
ahead of us. And who was I, driving and pulling
    the sound of death along with me,
who saw day taking into its new body
    the light lampposts cast on the highway?
I could not watch the miles so staked
    nor make a game of counting and keeping
in this month before your coming,
    when every machine was grinding, adjusting,

or pushing through the terrible heat,
        terrible, for which the lesser heat of the car
made me grateful: for sanctuary: to be in a place
        that had not exploded: outside
the music: to have you in me.

II

Project

Folding the paper in half.
Unfolding, smoothing it.

Finding the same gestures
for swans and boats.
Deciding.

Folding shadows into the head,
the whole swan around the dark
triangle of an eye.

The bird in the palm of the hand,
so small it must be
far away.

Starting the iris. Plaiting
the leaves to imitate
a ladder.

Cinching hard the waist of a wasp.
Elaborating. Balancing the wings
of a butterfly on two points
so light passes through
but not wind.

Standing the sun
upright on
its rays.

Giving the impression, with pleats,
of a caught fish thrashing in the beak
of a virtuosic pelican.

Turning corners by memory. Articulating points
around the center of a starfish. Three more
moves and the intermediary
bloom collapses
perfectly into
a beetle.

Thinking of what to call it midrun.
Finding how to lift the spotted head
by pressing along its back. Pinching
along the line of vertebrae.
Making it bark like that.

Milkweed

The petals dried to opening:

three lips,
inside, a scant few seeds,
the clusters beads
bell-bronze, no, light
enough to blow away,
pod and all, and land in the grass:

still green:
so strange in this freeze
as a brown rivulet down a stripped limb:

how the chalice of the squirrel
itself, the wetness of its own receiving,
disappears:

a heavy clapper sound
flies from, that sound rests in,
should it find a tiger lily's ear
so lent. See how wide the milk-
weed is open, those seeds,
those BBs sheened, see how
lips part for a delicacy:

a right word and its occasion—
barrage:

the squirrel's quick heart and the driving rain—
each makes itself a ravenous face,
a path for daring, flushed as bounty,

as the body is in bearing.

For Joseph, at Six Months

Though the leaves on the crooked tree,
heart-shaped, the size of my boy's head,
are quivering *silver-gone-green* and back,
the wind, with its common means, says
dark and *light*, then rustles down
to the healthiest bud—a star
because of its five ways out.
And water goes to the rampant vine,
knuckling in, dressing each step up.
This circling bee, indelicate song,
knows a way to sweetness.
It floats in the heat of its body.
It shudders in the face of abundance,
stunned for a moment at the entrance
to the shining city green is,
and is gone to purple aster. It finds
the rose blown wide. And today, because
I stepped out of his sight (did not exist
for a minute, for my boy), it moved
alone among the branches
of honeysuckle in his eyes.

Accident

Patience turned too sharply from
        suddenly became
                hackles on the mother cat,
                        a hangnail catching silk.

And getting up,
        a big mistake.
                Each butter knife a blade.
Then, heading to the cabinet,
        the wooden floor,
                askance.

Me on the ground, a toppled beam.
        My arm a joint pinned under.
And vast, the distance to the door,
        the door itself, a mouth,
                the sky beyond all toothy hail.

But then, the sun, refracted,
        honey in a jar.
A bowl of ice,
        a thawing stream.
My mind in there,
        metal unforging.
A glass of milk,

              the milk of ages.
The pocked, sad face of ground
        chamomile
                once again.
This purple cloud on skin,
        the shadow of a passing bird,
I mean
        the patience
                came back in.

Vigor Brand

It's there, in the eye of the running horse
on the orange crate, ears leaned back,
foam at the mouth, and tongue curled up.
It's in the muscle of the horse's neck, that rolling pin,
and the red of each nostril, the black mane lifting,
and carrot slip-knotted, hung almost in reach,
but the horse won't look, driving out of the frame.
Where is the light that startled him?
What is that sound in the air between us:
Grown and Packed in San Joaquin?
How does that mean inside are mountains
of pocked skin, bitter oil, moons in their phases?
There's a spot on the horse's muzzle—blue
as night descending, so blue the soft cheek
exaggerates what the horse keeps—a ball, a fist,
something that thrilled the eye and was taken,
it's taken an orange, and hiding it there,
the horse is sorry, the foam is a tear,
and yellow, slipped down the animal's chest,
is a sign of goodness, sun coming again
from *San Joaquin,* in hunger, in anger,
the outstretched neck tearing away
from representation, from being
the thing that distinguishes *these*
oranges from those the horse wants to leave,

and rounding a corner, it's running, not moving,
as in a bad dream, gold light on its tooth,
in its mouth the fire, sweet,
secret abundance the horse is afraid
of being, of holding.

Sketches and Models

I drew an eye in a field today
and knew the eye was an elephant's
by its deep intelligence which is earth- and glass-black
and too often overcome by the spectacle of its body.
I can't help finding in knots of wood
something that looks exactly back.
The deer's legs were fine
if drawn up in sleep, but next,
though I nearly turned away,
next came the amplitude of its ribs:
tatters of flesh, clean as good rags.
If the deer was already unweaving, the ribs
still worked to make a nest. A cage.
Crows came to eat. The ribs were eaves.

And once I saw a sculpture of a thin man
that I loved. It was not metal
eaten down to bone, but a man
whose vertebrae had trained the wind
to argue through him. I liked the excesses
of that, and thumbprints which were
each as an insult deeply felt.
They made a scaffold of fact, over which
the stunned garment of attitude fell.
And once a friend made, in a piece of music,

a transparent thing fly close, too close,
to the empirical transparency of a window.
Hit and be silent. Rev up again. Hit-rev,
and every time bring its silence
to an inconclusive end. I admired the way
the sound kept trying to meet itself in the other world—
and how the sky beyond wouldn't bend
or shift the blue bowl of itself any closer.

Here, where I sat down to work,
I found a cairn of four stones, angled
something like a family—a large, white
mother, the dark wedge of a father, and
two children who look most like each other.
I am tempted to say three are leaning on the mother,
that she is at the bottom and this late in the day
shadows and the weight of the others rest upon her.
Once this would have looked to me like a burden.
How easily balanced, though, they all seem—
depression to cleft, valley to upslope.

I tried sitting still in the changing light.
Tried to imitate the pile, but mine
looked like a peasant woman dragging
cockeyed, heavy sacks. For which she would get
not half the contents' worth.
I am grateful that something in my piece
invited me to knock it down.
It's getting toward evening.
Where each stone meets the other
is a thin, black line—

a seam, a road, its own
horizon. If I were to sketch it,
I would have to employ
sleights of hand, of shade and light,
for the good of holding everyone
so naturally together.

Beads

What crumb is the wasp eating, trapped
      days between windows, its body
two beads impossibly hinged, its body
      black beads, light on them a wetness, a shine,
a weight hoisted magnificent inches, all morning
      the wasp moves and falls back, moves and falls.

I hadn't suspected the terrible waist,
      that filament, was a breath
         between thoughts.

There was a time I did not think of the day
      as an animal come with a taste in its throat,
an ache in its side. I did not think my words would array,
      foreshorten the blizzard of an hour.
I thought an hour was no time to work. That the awful
      cicadas would always be with us.

Though every year before the cold
      is their armor forsaken, and the jade
         of their bodies unlaced.

Some Solaces

That switch-among-switches
once flowered magnolia.

It made the most
astonishing sound
in air.

※

And this, the same sun
that could not command itself
slant into barracks,
into such dark,

just now
struck the blade of a knife
blind.

※

Those bags of leaves
by the side of the road:
animals captured
and blaming themselves—

but look at the maple,
its uppermost branch
red-on-the-loose,
getting out, getting out—

Brown Leaf

It must have been tripped, it must have been shoved

and made to skitter, to mince away, this brown leaf

late spring, if I'm seeing correctly its

turning-for-nothing, its points eating air,

over the asphalt, over the curb, past trumpet-

gold daffodils, tulips in clusters,

forsythia heavy and wild and bent.

The way I came to the leaf was simple:

I was walking home from school.

You mean, the moment I learned to spot and name fear?

That it was faster, much faster than the maple out front

pushing forth little knives of green from its buds,

than the silk tips of pines

turning to needles,

is less important than knowing it was fear

I was seeing.

And once I saw it, fear was all over.

There among the perfect holes in the oak's trunk

where the woodpecker feeds, some of the holes

deeper than the rest, where a sweeter thing was found, and fear

that it would not be enough urged a deeper,

more violent digging in—

And among the staves of a basket, its dried, knotted reeds

lashed to hold water, and so to remember

once they were upright things and slender in a pond—

And I saw fear, too, in the way a pill bug coils

tightly when touched, then crawls fast to find the next heavy stone sky, which seemed sensible and right to believe in

—who would think of the sky lifting off? Yes

shaking, yes cracking with light, but the sky, which had been

a cool, pressing darkness, plucked cleanly away? Not that.

Sharp-clawed and frantic, the leaf turned over,

and over again until it hit the yellow

painted curb and could not move farther.

Pressed up against and fell back, pressed again,

was pushed down and lay there,

its edges turned up as if curled by a heat

held almost successfully off. As news-

papers will do when at first some meaning

can still be made out, before the whole

catches fire, folds in like a bowl. The leaf

itself was a bowl for fear, that conflagration

which in hunger, in turn, ate the bowl.

So what else could it have been

that I saw but the little cup

fear makes for pins, but a version of green

gone past its arc, brown-flecked, dun-silver,

a dry, nervous gallop fear keeps the reins to, sorry

thing in spring, this inclination

away from the bodies of others—

and though I would not have touched, less

hurt it—a leaf, a nothing!—had no intention

at all toward the thing, when I saw how it needed

me to name it, to say what I saw,

I stepped over. I gave it nothing

to be afraid of.

Pull

This fall, most branches went black in a smoke of gray leaves.

The thinnest branch imaginable balanced yellow

at its tip, and when the wind stopped, some clumps of leaves

were heavy pears. The squirrel pulled

one into his hands and began to chew:

hard to say *into its paws,*

he holds everything up

to his face so precisely.

A leaf blew hard into the screen and, on one of its points, stuck there.

It was spotted yellow and black and hunched like a beetle,

then rose on a draft, was the shape of a cup,

a teacup raised, but the draft returned and the cup fell down

and broke and was a yellow leaf again.

᠁

One morning my son said *Pull me! Down!*

and stretched his legs out on the bed, and waited, and watched.

Such song has been made of *pull* and *down*—

> . . . *Pull down thy vanity. I say pull down.*
> *Learn of the green world what can be thy place* . . .

But I knew on my face was a sickle of fear, a sharp moon

to shape into a smile for him.

᠁

Remember the man

pulled to death

behind a truck with a winch and a chain

to where death lay

in a cul-de-sac.

The dead man was stripped—

say *flensed* for a deer, or *skinned* for a coon,

⚶

say *stripped* of a title or a badge, dignity,

like going out without your name.

⚶

There are things that exist without a name—

The green, live scent
of an overgrown ditch.

The hollow place
in a man's hand where
an egg or chin would
fit.

⚶

No object is so attached to its name
that another cannot be found for it—

In my son's mouth, the word *pull* sounds like *pool*. A cool,

blue scene with a red bathing suit and a stitched honeybee.

But his word's a command: I should move his small body,

that sudden tonnage, bright in the sun as a rose-marble quarry, across the bed and rumpled quilt, blue as an aster, a whole

mottled field, blue as the scrim of integument,

blue my son calls the end of the day

when it comes with long fingers, the quiet of orchards,

when street lamps hum in the face of night

and stand immobile in yellow shirts.

Stunned Bird

From the far edge of thought
where I am mere
comes the larger breeze
of a larger thought—
a tree climbs the body of a bird into air—
and the bird in my hand
is a detonation, a stamp
of fire on the dawn-ushered day.
I hold it tighter,
as surely as it hopes to pass
this being guarded treasure,
someone's nimble love of costume.
I am waiting for its song,
though on my own
could pick the notes out
sweetly on an ocarina,
that fat bird's body, grimly hollow,
hollow as a fence post of sorrow
silvered in cold. I am waiting
for the bird's own version which is
more practiced, sure and clear.

Oh, little soul cosseted in black and red,
did I take you in, in faith,

to keep you from the hail, high wire,
bleaker plumage you would gather
as the months gather cold and colder?
Come. Eat from my hand.
What a kindness I impose—
deliberate attachment
to a hunger I've begun—
shining seeds of blackest oil,
water from a silver saucer.
How much more might you be fed
by the hunger that climbs you
into day, light winding along,
light in banks a share of silk
interposed between any bird
and its black cloak struck
red on the wing, a patch of it
fire-shocked, going on
appeasing my eye with its offhand
beauty, that terrible freight.

Grasses

Buffalo to steep in vodka,
to make the pulpy mind of summer swim.

Stiff rye for diamonds.
Cattails in the river.
Alfalfa in the horse's perfect dream.

Acres and acres
converted by bees.

On the news last night, torn apart
dark from dark
from flannel scrap,
good dogs root up
the buried boy:

A clipping in the pocket
of a trench.

Garlands of yellow tape
on the last-ditch bed.

And today
in a private green

expanse, bouquets
of stone. Stone words.
Stone lambs.

How the children
tried to say
goodbye
with dandelion chains.

The Boy's Story

The tree fell by pieces
    into the bed
        ivy, just for this occasion, made.

The trunk was wrecked. Struck,
    dumb segments were rickety steps,
        and green, jack-knifed,

cockeyed limbs bright
    where the cut ends shone
        like wet moons, wet faces.

What the boy saw in the open field
    through the gap where his favorite tree had been,
        what he saw rising up in place of his love

he wanted to name
    farthest castle, inner chamber. Then, when the sun
        was going down: *small candle in there.*

He wanted to see a boy in there. Looking back at him.
    But the saws had big teeth.
        The straps were leather.

He wanted to say: *I'll stand in waves of yellow wheat,*
          up to here. His small chest. No. This heat's shallow,
                    it rises from nothing. And falls, comes in hillocks,

fast in a way he cannot climb.
          Thick-limbed and once-petalled,
                    it is sawdust he stands in, this child

whose story has stopped, who stutters
          well then-then-then until he recovers
                    the splendor of saying,

of making by saying, of wanting
          to make it *all better,* of wanting
                    to make it be *ever after.*

He told of stray limbs and their overreaching. How the view was
          obscured and those good men came with good intentions,
                    but the trail of his story stopped there.

Where he veered.
          He walked and circled the empty spot,
                    kicked the bright colors piling up,

and closed his mouth
          to feel the red gap
                    where a tooth used to be.

Where his mouth filled with salt.
          And now, at the sight of the open field
                    the tree had been guarding,

its new growth off-
        shooting, as if the tree still
                had wild cares to attend—

there was no more hovering.
        The boy was crying.

Let it be known, the men had hearts
        of stone ground down, sharp
                teeth of silver,

and the noise of grinding
        followed them and they trod the green,
                their faces set against the edge of day,

set to work, to the ringing inside
        the cut trunk, the tolling—
                It took, the boy said,

oh he wanted to say,
        forever
                to bring the tree down.

III

Man's Work

A splendor is falling.
    A man bends close
to the tree he takes down—how sweet it must be
    before heat, before dust
spills from the machine in his hands.
    He is dressed in navy blue which means
to be darker than the water he once sailed upon,
    dark as the thought *whose blue,*
if not fought for, won over? Let me go back:
    This morning was tricked. Told it was nothing
more than his rising. Or mine. When I saw
    the man's arm through a break in the pines
pulling the cord so a voice, too, would rise,
    would flare and catch, and the white truck get to be
a bed for the sleep he was fashioning, how I wanted to say
    Oh here is someone not afraid of work!
How the marked trees accept such praise!
And the voice of the saw went darting
    after, riding up the bigger bodies,
and pitched still higher, into pink crape myrtle,
    made a wreck of grace, ash of a spine,
sheared the clotted blooms and they fell.
    In felling, the voice tore the morning asunder.
Logs piled up and the rise of cicadas, the whine of blades
    went over the quiet, that quiet voice he used as a boy,

a boy crawling under a fence calling *Wait!*
How the cut links snagged and he arched away
from the raking, cold metal, the light being brighter on the other side,
light, which, now that he's known such a thing, he can say
he was drunk on, wanted more of: that tippling gold
gone branched and cross-harrowed,
and nothing at all like its promise.
Now, in front of him, after his work,
there is the street, entirely visible.
The place the tree grew from glaringly open.
And those logs that were trees, they threaten the grass,
are blackening weather come to the grass,
smothering intention, heavy upon the hollow-tubed
shoots of onion, the snowdrops pinned
and likened to bells in their silence,
green weeds in a tangle, modest
and willing themselves from ruin.

Donkey Game

The sudden comes down,
the irrevocable, how
it flounders, it bangs
an announcement out.
Leaves in their gold
calamity—a party game!
Remember yourself with a tail
in your hand, moving blindfolded
toward the thing that had none?

How abrupt, like a night door,
how fast it came up, that swayed
brown back, tired of carrying.
How it stood in the bright
light, straight ears listening,
not twitching at flies or joy
because the sun was just right.
You bumped into it.

Blind eye to eye,
all that caressing—
how docile it was,
that stylized scream,
teeth and black mane,

all the tails in the air
falling, or clock hands, and you,
thinking *won't it hurt*
to complete it?

Red

If I let red
be the reward,

and the body of the bird
a medal for thought,

a medal that makes the next thought come:
the reddest red frays to gray underwing:

what, then, shall stand for its hail-colored secrets
and make the bird lift up again—what feeds

a rattling heart its beads of fear, so up
it tramples the corridor of air?

Let me calm the bird with smoke
—burning leaves, coming dusk—I keep

in my fire-stalking eye. Or the bird
will fly off to escape its own burning.

Stay with me. I am warming. I am working
on a song for the occasion. I watch

it eat and its black seed
of an eye. Seed it can't plant

away and be done with.
Reward for what?

For being surprised
a red bird in dull scraps keeps happening?

That it is winter, the bird is eating,
or trying to collect? It picks

and tosses dry bits aside,
which it could do, too, if merest brown,

a simple streaked sparrow, or wildly green.
But I watch because the bird is red,

my reason and my measure, and lush
beyond the season. Ripe already.

Its knife of feathers
is a cock's comb—the flower, I mean,

just a small spray though, soft and brief
and convoluted as a fiery brain.

The bush it is in will be forsythia
in a few more months, a yellow going

arm in arm with itself. And red then,
a truly fallen thing,

in collision, seen through stars of flowers,
reward for finding, at yellow's heart,

the bird's solitude and fear.
A reward is a startling thing.

Dance

Songs from far away are coming. They hum and gather.
How do they pass so safely through

the noose of each green link in the fence? No.
Each honeycomb—let it be—held wide open

as an eye for sweets, spare room
to move into, paper house

a breeze finds ripe to rifle. Let us,
wishing origins on things, say

mockingbird and *loon*. Bestow: a shapeliness
to keep it in. Bestow: intention. Then wishing more,

let us see the cinched waist of the wasp, close up
on the peeling sill, its hobbled tail a hinge still

moving, late at night, so late in the season. Let us hear
quadrille, flirtation in its slowing.

Portrait

A bird of ash
       spiraled up in
declaration: scent of burning,
       proclamation of the season:
so cold this blue
       must also mean
fire at its hottest.

At its hottest is how the jay
       took across the field just now
all it is and was: it pulled,
       it hauled along: sweet recitation
of hinge and plank, walls and eaves,
       until it entered, like despair,
this hollow house
       and clattered in
and made at least
       its awful cry
sit down
       and stay and flare.

Shadow

Drama in which a rose
is pinned to the ground.
In which thorns grow
like evening
into the tangle
of their own cage.

A black wing
added
to everything.

By noon
a perfect body
in decline.

Sun's hunger strike.
The very likeness
of dissent
growing
then gone.

What reason makes
of fear
in a solitary room.

Ground of being
from which the dark's
entire purpose is deduced.

First lesson in perspective:
dear architect,
your best effort
will lay itself down
in the street.

In fact, driving deeper into evening,
many things become fingers
and point the way.

But you, long tatter
at the foot of a tree,
boulder's train,
edge-of-the-woods cast
off the shoulder,
let me say

darkness becomes you.
And that plunging.

Though I Am Not

Though I am not Catholic I know
today is scented like a censer,
that a censer imitates cut-pine air,
the raw stump itself is the face of the moon,
and dark is what every day turns to.

And though I do not sit, contemplative, for long
before an idea about darkness comes,
I arrest it and keep it a few steps in front of me,
turned just so, as the deer turned one afternoon
that I might observe how ribs taper to a soft spot
before the haunch starts, how slack it goes there
and dim where the hide folds tenderly down the bone.
I might have seen where a bullet goes
but I made of that place a darkened window,
which is, of course, a mirror.

And though I am not the object its heart wants,
I know the brute machinery a hummingbird can be,
that it idles at the open hand of the blown rose,
and from that softened, debilitated pool
sips of the sweetest irony:
those who can't afford to give, do give. Give best.
It hovers lightly, a frenzy to me

because I must imagine hovering,
my body heavier now after my child.

My son is the scent of water from a silver cup.
I pour my face out willingly
that he might see there constancy,
for lingering near is the bounded
water of a puddle, trees face down in it,
trees spoking in, the marked sky and strop
of bird trail across, clouds winching along.

And though I don't know, I believe
the heart has a scent too,
which is the scorch love generates.
That the heart with its pistons
goes *climb up and step
down, climb-step, climb-step,* and
in this way the holy minutes go by,
whether you love your day or not.

Some Signs

The strawflower steeped in its gold inner face.
In my boy's open hand, a horse
chestnut, just cracked from its green, spiny pod,
a singular lump like a knuckle—
not taut-white with fear, but burnished
and darkened by labor.

The yellow roses, heavy, even as they climb the wet fence.
Even as they climb the wet fence, ants in a line
unzip those black hearts, sweet hearts blown open,
available, frayed—but tell me, how else
should a heart behave in the face of such devotion?

What else might a short life give signs of?
The end of everything already so near?
I know the end is news every day,
that green goes to dark lengths:
switch, kindling, horsewhip.
That yellow comes too, a fat pear, deep
as the cup of my hand: my child
ripe as the fruit I hold, the back of his head,
as he sleeps, a brown form perfectly still.

From lichen-covered rocks this comes:
what is massive is moved upon by years: those folds

in the tender slab of a boulder,
the fat-marbled rose face of a boulder.

Over this, the hawk idles, over this
the hawk cuts a sharp wing into hunger,
and toward it goes with its face of death
whatever form death likes today: small body
pushing leaves aside, itself calmly thinking
only of eating, which is, after all,
a sign of freedom.

Agreement

It looks like mutual agreement
between the wind and trees—
one turns away, the other
goes free.

On what is the agreement
written then—

the white-tipped wings
of the mockingbird
the heavy vine accepts
as harsh good
and necessary evil—
harvester, servant,
thief?

Hail's agreement:
water shall come
disguised as stone.
And soup agrees:
the blood of roots
will run together,
sweet, savory, and the pot
of the land shall be

all of yours to share.
Bread agrees to break.

In your dream, agree
to knit though you cannot knit.
Agree you never imagined
such grief and grieve.
Let green be the coat
of everything relentlessly alive.

This rock and that when
split down the middle
agree to produce a wall
of children between them.

And when the squirrel finally pries
the lid off the garbage can
and runs away, the lid clattering,
the squirrel up a tree,
its black claws and pounding heart,
luck, escape, let's agree,
that's gratitude raining
from the highest steady branch.

Cicada

For a week it's been spinning
the tale of a thing
about to believe
its new body.
Today the eyes are gone,
the center split
where form side-stepped
its own riven length.

That's just likeness
hinged to the tree.
A souvenir.
A transparency.

To find it now
make a space in the ear
in the shape of what it's become:

A thirst.
A flood.

Listen. Already
the ear
is the lip
of a generous cup.

Ribbon

Such flare from a scrap of ribbon!

Such an arc of revelation:

a back bent in sun, a banner of gold

caught on a twig, so bright it holds

the crow's eye and mine, holds itself ready

as a snake of poured metal, goes sifting in green

for an arm, for a neck,

as finery will, settling over good bones.

Years ago, such a light caught, too,

on pie plates I hung across the yard

to scare the crows and grackles away.

The plates were suns alarmed by wind,

extravagant when they tipped their rage up

into my face so I was sun-struck

and it hurt to look. I wanted to bang them

with a stick, for rough music,

or hold the stick high and think *I lit them*

and so could put them cruelly out.

But night did that.

Here, now, that wildest flare is fallen,

rolls, snags the fence, turns

dull in an instant as a hurt remembered.

Sips from the grasses' edge and dapples over.

What will I do with you now, little shine,

pretend to know where you came from? Listen:

the crimp of gold caught at the edge

at the end of winter, held in the scrub,

oh it beckons, suggests to the birds

how they need such a plateful, a mouthful: gold

for a floor. Gold for an entry. Bunting

of gold to wrap the smallest ones in

for warmth. And from the gold call

of goldfinches, I know embellishment

is a devilish song, a seduction,

not that staggering, frayed peony, not

real sadness, regret, or my body,

or once, as I put it, *Are you ok?*

Do you need money?

That I might make of the outrage I was

a flower

no one will see.

That I might use the ornament I found

for nothing. For thatching. And build a house

of light and air, the nothing

I would give you now, increase

of this fine day alone. Here:

let this be, my old friend,

your bent back the sun is finding.

Room

In this time left, let light prop
        the body troubling to stay
upright. Let the overflow
        catch and keep, in a barrel
like rain, for shine, for feed.
        Casual as snow, let late sun
come into the fray, make a window
        on the apple's rump.
The apple on the wooden tray.
        Let me, the falling sound
in the orchard, be hurried by one
        whose name I call,
by yellow rays across the room,
        a water glass with gashes of ice.
The book I left an hour ago, the lacing of
        its perfect spine, so close.

Tree

Where the branches crossed and tied/untied a net,
where the net of branches startled and broke into many Ms,
more partial still—I could see very clearly—Ns, I could see

⚎

the net failing, gaps pull apart where air winged
through and spread the strands farther,

⚎

shifted the catch, left the sky ragged—

⚎

I saw the tree hold, in its restless arms, the whole
of the alphabet, how the silver limbs gathered
to furnish a word of their own for *rustle*.

⚎

I saw, too, that I owned the tree. And had I been feeling
Romantic, would have chafed at that notion, would have seen
candelabra, blooms the wind lit, each bud in its singular vase.

⚎

But I thought—
it will be mine

to gather up when they fall,
dry slips, little curls, in the cold.

⚔

When my friend's tall beauty cracked last year
in a storm, he sold it, the wood, for five hundred dollars.
What he called *paulownia* hung over his porch
and reached with thick purples, late spring, to his table.
He pulled the flowers out of air and shaped their bodies, telling me.
It was how an icicle melts that I saw, or a bull's horn, saber, fetlock
   form.
A cornucopia overflows, an eggplant tapers at the neck.

⚔

And because of what he owned once, his hands
made a shapely thought to see,
and when there was nothing again in his palm
but a ribbon of pulse, his fingers and thumb
came together to rest on the table.

⚔

I have not told that I own this tree. Not told of it
to anyone, much less the tree itself.
It is true I come out to our new yard to watch it,
to get an eyeful of crosshatch and furrow, fringe
sheer in the sun, a sigh roughed in,
but I've said
no more to myself than

Look
isn't its fretwork

a menace
a windfall?

⚔

I have not yet made
of the tree a place
my ownership offends.

⚔

And really,
whatever the wind
says the tree is, the tree is—
the wind paring its thoughts
sparing nothing at all,
going in with its white,
with its perfect blade.

NOTES

The book's epigraph is from *The Solace of Open Spaces* by Gretel Ehrlich (New York: Viking, 1985).

Lines 17 and 18 of "Pull" are taken from Ezra Pound's Canto LXXXI. Lines 30, 37, and 38 adapt language from the writing of Max Ernst.

The Ohio State University Press /
The Journal Award in Poetry

DAVID CITINO, POETRY EDITOR

The George Elliston Poetry Prize